SCOTLAND

LISA PRITCHARD

MYRIAD
LONDON

Jedburgh *below*

The Royal Burgh of Jedburgh is just 10 miles from the border with England. Known as the "Jewel of the Scottish Borders", the town is famous for the ruined Jedburgh Abbey, situated on the north bank of Jed Water. The abbey church was the main place of worship until Trinity church in the high street was established.

Leaderfoot Viaduct, Melrose

The magnificent 13-arch Leaderfoot Viaduct crosses the river Tweed a few miles east of Melrose. Built in 1865, it once carried a section of the Berwickshire railway which closed in 1948. It is now part of the Tweed Cycle Way, an 89-mile long cycle trail which starts at Biggar and finishes at the coast at Berwick-upon-Tweed.

Abbotsford *left*

On the south bank of the Tweed near Melrose, the spectacular Abbotsford is a historic house which was formerly the home of the novelist Sir Walter Scott (1771-1832). The son of an Edinburgh solicitor, Scott was a literary sensation and the author of many bestselling novels. Abbotsford, which is often likened to a "fairy palace", is rich in oak and cedar panelling, is decorated with heraldic symbols and contains many suits of armour, hunting trophies and items of military history, including Rob Roy's sword. The house, with its beautiful garden, is open to the public.

Tantallon Castle *above*

This stronghold was the first major obstacle
any army venturing across Scotland's
easternmost border would have encountered.
Tantallon Castle is just three miles from North
Berwick and its position on top of a high cliff
gives it an unimpeded view of the Bass Rock
in the Firth of Forth. Built in 1358, Tantallon's
fortunes finally declined in 1651 when
Cromwell destroyed it while rooting out
bandits who had been using it as a base.

St Abb's Head *left and below*

The rocky outcrop and harbour of St Abb's
Head in Berwickshire is the point at which the
British coastline takes a sharp turn to the left
and heads west into the Firth of Forth – until
this point it had generally headed north.
It was the sinking of a ship called *The Martello*
in 1857 that prompted the building of the
lighthouse here in 1862. The engineers were
the famous David and Thomas Stevenson,
who also built the lighthouse at Douglas
Head, on the Isle of Man.

Melrose Abbey *left*

Two miles to the west of
Melrose, on the south side of
the Tweed, lie the magnificent
ruins of Melrose Abbey. This
Cistercian abbey dates from
1136 when monks from
Rievaulx in north Yorkshire
founded the monastery at the
request of King David I of
Scotland. In 1322 the abbey
was attacked by the English
army of Edward II and much
of the building was destroyed.
The generosity of Robert
the Bruce allowed for the
rebuilding of the abbey; on
his death, Robert's embalmed
heart was buried there. In
1544 the abbey was again
damaged, this time by the
armies of Henry VIII. Today
the abbey is under the care of
Historic Scotland.

Edinburgh

The beautiful city of Edinburgh has been the capital since 1437 and the castle, perched on its volcanic crag, dominates its surroundings. One of the most popular views of the city is from Calton Hill where the panorama (right) sweeps across the Old Town to the castle. The Royal Mile descends from the castle to the Palace of Holyrood and contains many famous buildings including St Giles Cathedral and the splendid new Scottish Parliament. Edinburgh's most famous thoroughfare is actually a little more than a mile in length and is made up of a number of historic streets including Castlehill, Lawnmarket, High Street, Canongate and Abbey Strand which leads to the Palace of Holyrood. In the 17th century this was an area of overcrowded tenement buildings, some of which were 14 storeys high. There were as many as 70,000 people living in this part of the city, making it insanitary and disease-ridden. In the late 19th century, the Lord Provost William Chambers and the town planner Patrick Geddes re-modelled the area and laid out courtyards and gardens which echoed the design of the medieval city with its narrow alleyways (known as closes) and open squares, which were used originally to house animals. Today this elegant and attractive quarter is chock full of shops, restaurants and cafes and is a magnet for visitors.

The Military Tattoo

Every August the city hosts a magnificent festival of arts, music and drama. One of the highlights is the annual Edinburgh Military Tattoo (below), when the castle esplanade is packed with spectators. Massed pipes and drums vie with military marching bands and Highland dancers, and in the closing moments a lone piper plays a lament on the castle ramparts.

The Palace of Holyroodhouse

The Queen's official residence in Scotland, Holyroodhouse began life as a monastery in 1128. It has witnessed many turbulent events in Scottish history, and was home to Mary Queen of Scots between 1561-1567. Today the Palace is used for official entertaining, state ceremonies and garden parties; it is open to the public at certain times.

Princes Street *below*

There is something for everyone in Princes Street – fashionable shops and the Princes Street Gardens along the south side, complete with a funfair and ice rink at Christmas; the monument (right of photograph) to Scotland's favourite author Sir Walter Scott and his dog. It runs parallel to the famous Royal Mile, which has linked Holyroodhouse with Edinburgh Castle since the Middle Ages. Many of Edinburgh's key attractions lie along these two thoroughfares.

Forth Bridges *above and below*

In Alfred Hitchcock's thriller *The 39 Steps* the hero escapes from a train on the Forth railway bridge (above) to dangle 150ft (45m) above the chilly waters of the Firth of Forth. In 1890 this dramatic structure was the world's first major steel bridge. It still carries over 180 trains a day along the east coast to and from Edinburgh. Such a huge structure – the central span is over 1100 yards (1km) long – has inevitably required continuous maintenance, and "painting the Forth Bridge" became a metaphor for an endless (and unrewarding) task. But new technology now means it will only need to be repainted every 30 years. Seen from South Queensferry, the graceful suspension road bridge (below left of photograph) that opened in 1964 complements the solid cantilever rail bridge. It replaced the centuries-old ferries which crossed the river.

Pittenweem *below*

This pretty seaside village is viewed here from the outer harbour wall close to an assortment of lobster and crab traps. Pittenweem's name derives from the Scottish Gaelic and is thought to mean "the place of the cave". The cave in question is probably nearby St Fillan's cave, although there are many other candidates along this indented shoreline. The white village houses with red roofs shown in the photograph illustrate the classic East Neuk of Fife building style, influenced by trade with the Low Countries of Belgium and the Netherlands.

Bass Rock *top*

One of the world's best examples of a volcanic plug, the Bass Rock rises about 100ft (30m) out of the Firth of Forth. Some 40,000 pairs of gannets shelter and nest here, and from the coast the rock appears white thanks to their guano and their characteristic markings. The castle on Bass Rock was built by the Lauder family in the 15th century, who lost it during the Civil War.

Elie *above*

It may look like the ancient remains of an abbey or castle but the structure overlooking the magnificent vista at Elie in Fife is actually an 18th-century folly. The Lady's Tower was built to serve as a dressing room for Lady Anstruther, an early naturist, who used to bathe naked in pools nearby while a servant tolled a bell to warn locals to keep away.

Crail *right*

The most easterly of Fife's fishing ports, this tranquil village was first granted its royal charter by Robert the Bruce in 1310. Crail harbour is one of the oldest and the best in the area and there was trading with the Continent as far back as the 9th century. Traces of this link can be seen in the town's architecture, some of which has a Dutch influence, and in the town's medieval marketplace, one of the largest in Europe.

Stirling *left and inset*

The childhood home of Mary Queen of Scots, Stirling is the grandest castle in Scotland. It looms over the scene of some of the nation's most important battles and was frequently besieged as England fought to dominate the Scottish kingdom. In 1297 William Wallace triumphed over Edward I's army at Stirling Bridge. Seventeen years later the English were once again defeated by Robert the Bruce at Bannockburn. Stirling is also home to the Wallace Monument which celebrates William Wallace and his pivotal role in Scotland's struggle for independence. Though he never won another battle, his execution for treason in 1305 succeeded in stoking the Scots' determination to achieve independence. Robert the Bruce was crowned king at Scone the following year.

Loch Lomond *left and above*

The Loch Lomond and the Trossachs National Park was created in 2002 and is the fourth largest national park in the British Isles. Loch Lomond lies 20 miles north-west of Glasgow and is Britain's largest freshwater loch, 24 miles long and five miles wide. Most visitors hope to catch the classic view of the loch's mirror-like waters reflecting the snow-capped peak of Ben Lomond (above) from the pier in the village of Luss. Loch Arklet (left) near Inversaid was enlarged by the building of a dam to supply Glasgow with water in the early years of the 20th century. Along its shore lies Corriearklet Farm where Rob Roy was married.

Blair Castle *above*

The ancient seat of the Dukes and Earls of Atholl, the imposing Blair Castle is located in Glengarry, guarding the route north to Inverness. The castle is the home of the Atholl Highlanders, Europe's last remaining private army. The regiment had been disbanded in 1783 but in 1839 the Duke resurrected it as a ceremonial guard; it was given its colours by Queen Victoria in 1844 when she visited the castle.

Callander *left*

The town of Callander on the river Teith is the eastern gateway to the Loch Lomond and the Trossachs National Park. The Callander Crags dominate the town to the north; there are beautiful views from the summit over the town and across Loch Venachar.

St Monans *above*

Along the coast from Pittenweem, the picturesque fishing village of St Monans is situated on a hill overlooking the Firth of Forth, with views to North Berwick, the Bass Rock and the Isle of May. The dramatic 14th-century St Monans church sits on a jagged cliff above the water's edge on the west side of the town. Built by David II, the only son of Robert the Bruce, the church commemorates the king's miraculous recovery from an arrow wound sustained at the battle of Neville's Cross in 1346.

Comrie *left*

Five miles west of Crieff the attractive village of Comrie is known as "the Shaky Toun" because of its position on an ancient fault line, which gives rise to occasional earth tremors. Its distinctive White Church, a listed building, is now used as a community centre.

St Andrews

The centre of St Andrews still shows its medieval origins, when it was Scotland's religious and intellectual hub. St Andrews University is the third oldest in the UK, dating from 1410, and it is widely considered to be one of Scotland's best. Its School of Divinity is still housed in the original 16th-century buildings of St Mary's College. For a panoramic view of St Andrews Cathedral (above) and the town beyond you can climb St Rule's Tower. The vast cathedral was consecrated in 1390, when Robert the Bruce is said to have ridden up the aisle on a horse. In 1559 the Reformist John Knox, founder of the Church of Scotland, so stirred up a mob with his fiery oratory against "popery" that they tore down the cathedral, leaving the ruins you see today.

Golfers everywhere consider St Andrews as the home of golf. For more than 250 years the Royal and Ancient Golf Club has been the arbiter of the rules of the sport. One of the most well-known sights of the course is the famous old bridge over the Swilken Burn (below left) which is crossed by all the world's golfing greats when the British Open Championship is held at St Andrews.

Glenfinnan

Beautiful Glenfinnan is an area rich in Scottish history. It was here that Charles Edward Stuart raised the Royal Standard, the spark which lit the 1745 Jacobite rebellion. The Glenfinnan Monument (left), on the shores of Loch Shiel, commemorates the Highlanders who perished for the cause.

The calm waters of Loch Eilt (above) was one of the locations used in the film *Harry Potter and the Prisoner of Azkaban* in the scene where Hagrid skims stones on the lake. It is an ideal spot for fishing and in the past had a reputation as one of the top Scottish sea trout lochs.

The Glenfinnan Viaduct (below) was built between 1897 and 1901. It carries passengers on the West Highland Line which runs between Fort William and the fishing villages of Arisaig and Mallaig. It too featured in a Harry Potter film, *Harry Potter and the Chamber of Secrets*, where the steam train was transformed into the Hogwarts Express and was filmed crossing the viaduct.

Tayside

The prow of *The Unicorn*, a 46-gun frigate built in 1824, frames this photograph of Dundee (above) while in the background stands Scott's *Discovery*. Both ships are testament to the long history of shipbuilding here on the north bank of the Tay. The river flows through some of the most beautiful glens in central Scotland. Seen here is the historic and picturesque Loch Dochart (above left) which lies on the upper reaches of the river, just east of Crianlarich.

North of Dundee lies the majestic Glamis Castle (left), the childhood home of the Queen Mother and the birthplace of Princess Margaret.

Just outside Perth is Scone, the ancient place of coronation of the Scottish monarchy. The monarchs were crowned on the Hill of Credulity, the present Moot Hill in the grounds of Scone Palace where a small chapel now stands (below).

Fraserburgh *above*

Forty miles north-east of Aberdeen, the beautiful beach at Fraserburgh is popular with walkers and holidaymakers. The Fraser family bought up much of the surrounding area in the late 16th century and their castle was converted into Scotland's first mainland lighthouse in 1787, renamed Kinnaird Head Lighthouse. Close by is the Museum of Scottish Lighthouses and the Fraserburgh heritage centre.

Dunnottar Castle *below*

The ruins of the medieval fortress of Dunnottar Castle, near Stonehaven, stand guard over the sea. This was home to the Keith clan and was used as a secure place in times of strife for the Scottish crown jewels. The ruins are spread over a three acre area virtually surrounded by 160ft (50m) high sheer cliffs. In 1990 Dunnottar was used as the key location in the Mel Gibson and Glenn Close screen version of *Hamlet*.

Aberdeen South Pier *left*

A massive wave crashes into Aberdeen's South Pier, driven on by storms in the North Sea. The 1050ft (320m) breakwater with the Girdle Ness Lighthouse, built in 1833, are both almost entirely obscured by spray on such days. Aberdeen Harbour, designed by John Smeaton and Thomas Telford, is a triumph of civil engineering. The city's docks are as important as they have ever been, playing a crucial role in the supply and support of the North Sea oilfields. Aberdeen is the principal commercial port in northern Scotland and an international port for general cargo and container traffic.

Cruden Bay *below*

The romantic Dunbury rock arch sits just off the Aberdeenshire coast near the village of Cruden Bay. In 1012 the settlement was the site of a battle between the Scots and invading Scandinavian raiders; it is thought that its name derives from the Gaelic for "slaughter of Danes". Today, Cruden Bay attracts tourists with its hotels and golf course.

Deeside

The magnificent royal residence and estate of Balmoral (left) is situated in the Dee valley, west of Aberdeen. It is the summer home of the Queen and the Duke of Edinburgh. Its royal connection dates back to 1848 when the house was first rented to Queen Victoria and Prince Albert. The royal couple enjoyed Deeside so much that they bought the house and immediately began a substantial programme of improvement and renovation.

Also on Deeside, just east of Banchory, lies the fairytale Crathes Castle (above). Built between 1553 and 1596, this perfectly preserved fortified house was presented to the nation in 1951 and is now under the care of the National Trust for Scotland.

Glen Coe

If you are walking the challenging West Highland Way, you come to the wilds of Rannoch Moor (above) with its rocks, lochs and mountains – here you see Ba Loch with Black Mount in the background. Where Glen Etive meets the pass of Glen Coe, Stob Dearg (above right) rises at the end of the Buachaille Etive Mor ridge. This peak is a favourite with walkers and climbers of all abilities.

Many people still feel a frisson as they enter Glen Coe, an echo of the horrific massacre of the Clan MacDonald in January 1692. The MacDonalds had given their traditional rivals, the Campbells, shelter for 10 days before their guests turned on them on the order of King William III. Many of those who escaped died of hunger and exposure in the surrounding hills.

Today Glen Coe is promoted as "the cradle of Scottish mountaineering". The history of the glen and the surrounding area is recorded at the eco-friendly Glencoe Visitor Centre (left) at the western end of the glen. The centre, which is run by the Scottish National Trust, opened in 2002; it contains a fascinating exhibition entitled "Living on the Edge" featuring the area's ecology, heritage and climbing history.

Caledonian Canal *left*

The Caledonian Canal links north-east and south-west Scotland, running through the Great Glen from Inverness to Corpach, near Fort William. The canal is seen here close to the last set of locks at Corpach, with Ben Nevis in the background. Sixty miles in length, for 38 miles it utilises the waters of Loch Lochy, Loch Oich and Loch Ness. Along its length there are 29 locks.

Kilchurn Castle *right*

The romantic ruins of Kilchurn Castle stand at the north-east end of Loch Awe. It was built in about 1450 by Sir Colin Campbell, first Lord of Glenlochy. At the end of the 17th century the house was converted into modern barracks, capable of housing 200 troops, and was used as a government garrison during the Jacobite rebellions of 1715 and 1745.

Loch Ness

You will probably not spot the legendary monster in the beautiful waters of Loch Ness that stretch from Inverness to Fort Augustus, but you are certain to see a wide variety of birds – if you are lucky you may even see an osprey fishing for salmon or brown trout. The view down the loch (below) from Dores on the south bank gives an idea of its sweeping grandeur. Six major rivers flow into this deep, long loch, and the short river Ness in turn drains the water into the sea at Inverness. By Drumnadrochit on the north bank, the ruins of Castle Urquhart sit on Strone Point (above and above left). This used to be the largest of all Scotland's castles: it was much enlarged by the English King Edward I. In his continuing efforts to subdue the country he became known as the Hammer of the Scots.

Fort Augustus *above*

At the southern end of Loch Ness lies Fort Augustus. Boats must pass through the lock to enter the Caledonian Canal, which continues to Fort William via the spectacular Neptune's Staircase locks.

Corran Narrows Lighthouse *below*

The lighthouse at Corran Narrows at the southern end of Loch Linnhe was built in 1860 to allow safe passage at night through the bottleneck of the narrows. This stretch of water was increasingly being used by larger ships due to the expansion of the paper industry in Fort William.

Inverness and Culloden

Inverness is often called the Capital of the Highlands. The surrounding region has the lowest population density in Europe, but this is one of Europe's fastest growing cities. Its castle (right), on the banks of the river Ness, was built in the 1830s, not to subdue the town but to run it and to house the law courts.

Greig Street footbridge (below) is one of several bridges that span the river Ness and Caledonian Canal in Inverness as they approach the Moray Firth. Thomas Telford built the canal to link the North Sea and the Irish Sea.

For a thought-provoking piece of Highland history visit Culloden Moor (below right), the site of the last land battle fought in Britain. You can walk round the battlefield where the hopes of Bonnie Prince Charlie, the pretender to the British throne, and his Jacobite army were savagely shattered in 1746 by the Duke of Cumberland's army. The bloody battle lasted just an hour but the story of the prince's escape to France was told for generations. Some of his wounded followers were less fortunate: they took refuge in a barn at Old Leanach farm only to be killed by Cumberland's men.

Dalwhinnie *above*

The distillery at Dalwhinnie is the highest in Scotland, at 1160ft (358m). The white-painted buildings are clearly visible on the western side of the A9 at the head of Loch Ericht. The distillery was originally an inn which served the needs of cattle drovers taking their animals to the market at Crieff.

Cawdor *left*

This ancient castle east of Inverness was built as a private fortress by the Thanes of Cawdor in the late 14th century. The legend is that the Thane of Cawdor released a donkey loaded with gold and built the castle where it first stopped – in this case by a juicy holly-tree. The castle has remained in the possession of the Cawdor family for over 600 years, but it took its present form mainly in the 17th century. Although the castle is associated with Shakespeare's play *Macbeth*, it did not exist when the real Macbeth was alive in the late 11th century. The castle does, however, boast two ghosts.

Duncansby Head *below*

Near the inland village of John O'Groats, Duncansby Head, with its remarkable stacks, is the most northerly spot on the north-east coast of Scotland. The Stacks of Duncansby and Thirle Door Arch are truly dramatic. Duncansby Head is also the site of a lighthouse built in 1924. This beautiful stretch of coastline is reached via a single-track road from John O'Groats; on arrival, visitors are rewarded with views north over Orkney and west to Dunnet Head, the most northerly point on mainland Britain. A short walk behind the lighthouse and the view opens up to the south, over the distinctive Stacks and the Arch.

Hoy *above left and above*

Hoy, the second largest of the Orkney Islands, is seen (above left) from Mainland, the largest of the group. One of the most distinctive natural features in the British Isles, the Old Man of Hoy (above) is a sandstone rock stack rising from the sea to a height of 450ft (137m) off the west coast of the island. It is considered a classic challenge by rock climbers. The first successful ascent was televised in 1966. Modern techniques and equipment, however, have made it more accessible to slightly less experienced climbers and it has now been conquered many times.

Eshaness *left*

The district of Eshaness at the western tip of Northmavine contains some of the most spectacular sights in all Shetland. Here giant Atlantic rollers smash into black cliffs and the sea has carved a set of precipitous stacks, most notably the Drongs and Dore Holm, an awesome natural arch.

Skara Brae *inset*

The photograph suggests something of the extraordinary scale of this Neolithic village, located on the west coast of Mainland, Orkney. Skara Brae, which has been designated as a World Heritage Site, lay hidden for thousands of years until a great storm in 1850 blew away the sand and grass that had enveloped it. Early excavation up until 1868 revealed the impressive remains of four ancient buildings.

Arisaig *top*

The silver sands of the glorious beach at Arisaig, to the west of Fort William, overlook Loch nan Ceall, the "loch of the churches". In 1746 two French ships, sent to help the Jacobites after the Battle of Culloden, were engaged in battle with the Royal Navy in the loch. The pier at Arisaig is the summer terminus for trips to Eigg, Muck and Rhum. The village is a stop on the romantically named "Road to the Isles", and visitors who take this route will be entranced by the views of the islands.

Ullapool *above*

The beautiful west coast fishing village and resort of Ullapool is situated on the eastern shore of Loch Broom (right); further along that same shore lies the port of Ullapool, a centre of herring fishing following its founding in 1788. Its harbour was designed by Thomas Telford and is still in use today as a yachting haven and ferry port for traffic to the Outer Hebrides. Ullapool has a strong reputation as a centre of music and performance, particularly during the summer months.

Oban *above*

Known as "the Gateway to the Isles" the beautiful resort town of Oban, on the west coast of Scotland, is the principal port for the Western Isles with ferry services to Colonsay, Barra, Tiree and South Uist. Its importance was enhanced in 1880 with the coming of the railways. The town itself lies in a beautiful setting on Oban Bay and boasts a number of interesting buildings including McCaig's Tower which, like a coronet of stone, contains nothing more than the top of the hill on which it stands.

Plockton *left*

Looking due north over the seaward end of Loch Carron on the north-west coast of Scotland is the pretty village of Plockton. This was a planned village established in the 18th century in an attempt to stem the flood of Scottish emigration. The village is a popular tourist resort, especially since it was chosen as the location of the television series *Hamish Macbeth*. Nearby is Duncraig Castle, a 19th-century stately home built by the Matheson family.

Kyle of Lochalsh *above*

The village of Kyle received the greatest boost to its prosperity first with a road from Inverness in 1819 and then the coming of the railway in 1897. The rail connection from Kyle to Inverness is regarded as one of the most picturesque in Britain. In summer, steam trains attract rail enthusiasts who take the scenic route north through Achnasheen and Loch Carron. The most prominent building in Kyle is the Lochalsh Hotel with its slipway; until 1995 visitors could catch ferries here to the Isle of Skye before the road bridge was built. Kyle was also the main ferryport to Stornoway in the Western Isles but the shorter route from Ullapool was more favoured by travellers and the Kyle crossing was axed. Despite the loss of these two important ferries, Kyle is an attractive stopping-off point for visitors.

Old Man of Storr *above*

There are few more famous spots in western Scotland than the Storr, a rocky hill on the Trotternish peninsula overlooking the Sound of Raasay. The hill consists of a number of wonderfully shaped pinnacles or volcanic plugs.

Portree *below*

Portree is the main town on Skye. Its name comes from the Gaelic Port-an-Righ, or "King's Port" and this dates back to a visit by King James V who arrived with a fleet of ships in 1540 demanding that the island support him. One of the town's most important buildings is the Royal Hotel, the site of Bonnie Prince Charlie's farewell to Flora MacDonald in 1746. He would never see Scotland again. Many Scots would also leave Portree never to return – the start of their long haul to America and Canada. Modern Portree offers visitors many attractions including its own immediate surroundings and the nearby "Lump", as the peninsula south of the town is called.

The Cuillins *left*

This photograph across Loch Scavaig shows the Cuillins in all their magnificence. They have been described as the most dramatic range in Britain.

South Uist *below centre*

The standing stone at Pollachar on the south coast of South Uist (the second largest of the Western Isles) stands like a silent watcher over the Sound of Barra with the islands of Eriskay and Barra in the distance. It is a reminder of the ancient Celtic traditions and culture on these islands that still run deep today. Despite its small size – South Uist is only 22 miles north to south and seven miles wide – it enjoys a wide variety of scenery including an almost unbroken stretch of beach on the west coast and substantial mountains in the east which, in the case of Beinn Mhor, rise to 2033ft (620m).

Tobermory Harbour *above*

Tobermory means "Mary's Well" in Gaelic. The capital of the Isle of Mull, it is located on a superb natural harbour, and was developed as a planned fishing town by the British Fisheries Society. Many buildings in Tobermory, particularly shops and restaurants, are painted in assorted bright colours, making it a popular location for television programmes, including the children's show *Balamory*. It is also famous by association with the Wombles, one of whom was named Tobermory.

Harris

The photograph (above) is of the west coast of South Harris, the side that faces the North Atlantic and which is blessed with some of the best beaches in Scotland. South Harris, as can be seen from the view (below) across Loch Leosavay, is rugged. Among its main settlements is Rodel with the medieval kirk of St Clement's. One of the main tourist routes on Harris is the "Golden Road", which hugs the south-east coast from Tarbert to Rodel. It is so-named because of the high cost of its construction through difficult terrain.

South Harris is famed for its beaches and the largest and arguably the best is Luskentyre (below right). It lies near the narrow isthmus that connects North and South Harris. At high tide much of the bay is submerged, becoming part of the Sound of Taransay. Here the breathtaking view shows the island of Taransay in the distance.

Iona Abbey *left*

The Isle of Iona lies just a mile off the western tip of the Isle of Mull. Due to its association with St Columba, who established a monastery here in 563, it has long been a centre of Christianity and pilgrimage. The abbey, which is also the burial place of the early Scottish kings, was originally a medieval Benedictine foundation; today it is one of Scotland's most historic and venerated sites.

Rhum *above*

The rocky peaks of the Rhum Cuillin seen from the Bay of Laig on the island of Eigg, looking across the Sound of Rhum.

Dunvaig Castle *right*

Situated on the rugged shores of Islay, Dunvaig Castle was once a major stronghold. In the 17th century it was fought over by Alasdair "Old" Colkitto MacDonald, first with the Campbells of Cawdor and then with the Covenanting Army under David Leslie (1601-82). Leslie took the castle following a siege. The Campbells then occupied the castle until the 1670s when Sir Hugh Campbell demolished it and moved to the more comfortable Islay House nearby.

Glasgow

In recent years Glasgow has become a major player on the culture trail – it is no longer a byword for grit and grime, but a vibrant international centre. Leading the way is the Scottish Exhibition and Conference Centre (above) located on the north bank of the Clyde. The recently renovated Rotunda (above left) at the entrance to the harbour tunnel, is now a stylish restaurant while the 1904 Willow Tea Rooms (above the jewellers), in Sauchiehall Street, designed by Charles Rennie Mackintosh, remain a style icon. At the heart of Glasgow is George Square (above right) with statues of Scotland's greats including Robert Burns, James Watt and Sir Walter Scott. The river Clyde (left) was key to Glasgow's commercial prominence as a port and textile centre in the 18th and 19th centuries.

Kelvingrove Art Gallery and Museum (right) is the Glaswegians' favourite Edwardian building, and the most visited museum in the UK outside London. The building itself is in a Spanish Baroque style, and its wide-ranging collections include major Impressionist paintings.

Isle of Arran

Lying in the Firth of Clyde, Arran is the seventh largest Scottish island. Often referred to as "Scotland in miniature" it is divided into highland and lowland areas. Lochranza Castle, a hunting lodge of Scottish kings, is in the north.

Ailsa Craig *right*

The conical shape of Ailsa Craig is seen here next to the low-lying island of Pladda. It is the place where curling stones are quarried.

Portpatrick *below*

This pretty village clings to the south-westerly tip of Scotland on the Rhins of Galloway.

First published in 2009
by Myriad Books Limited,
35 Bishopsthorpe Road,
London SE26 4PA

Photographs copyright © Britain on View,
the image resource centre of Visit Britain

Text copyright © Jerome Monahan

Jerome Monahan has asserted his right under the Copyright, Designs and Patents Act 1998 to be identified as the author of this work.

ISBN 1 84746 250 2

EAN 978 1 84746 250 3

Designed by Jerry Goldie Graphic Design

Printed in China

www.myriadbooks.com